I0485550

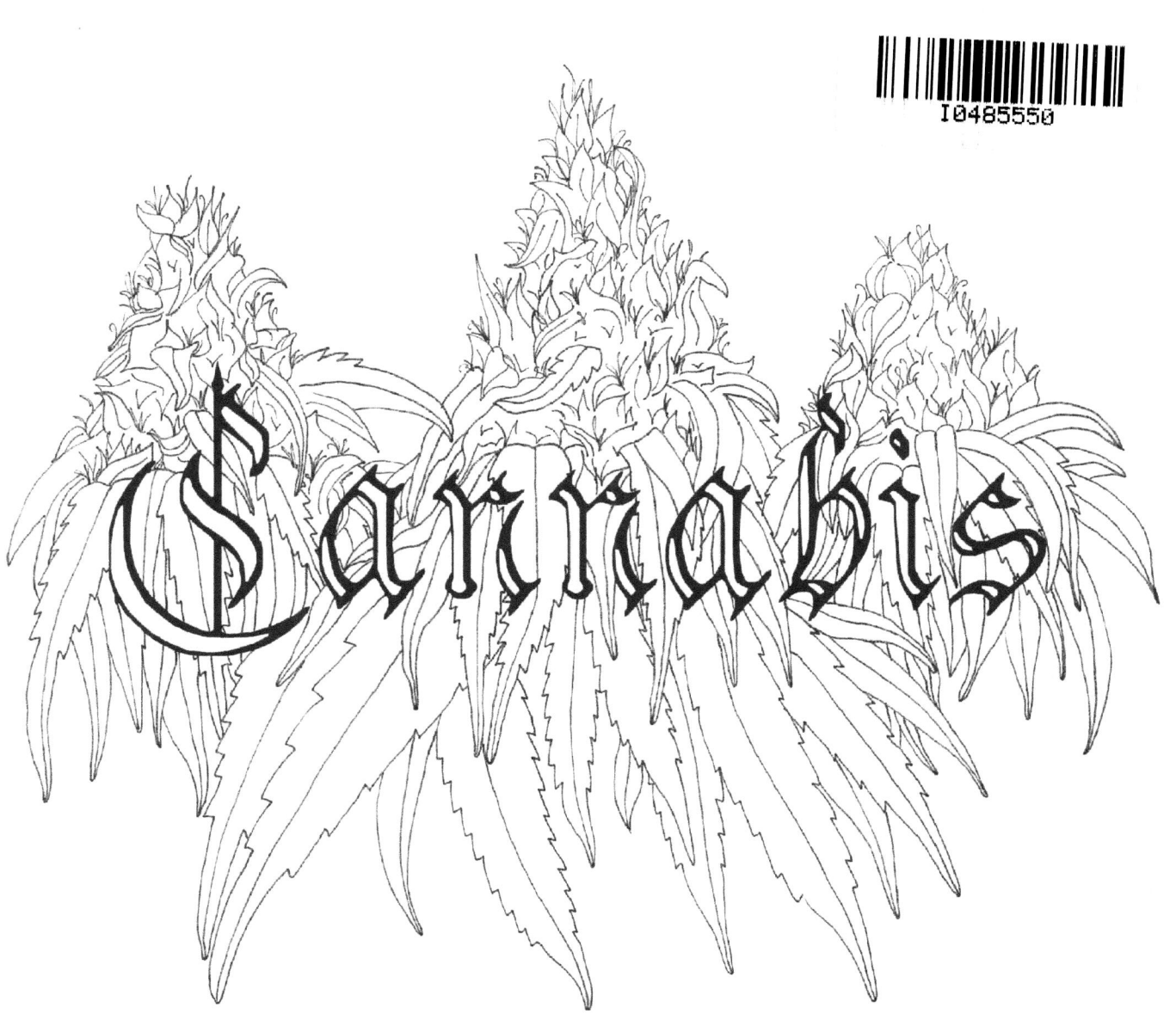

Colorado

Adult Coloring Book

Inspired designs from our own Cannabis garden.
We hope you enjoy coloring these as much as
we enjoyed creating them.

The proceeds of this coloring book help support Colorado Cannabis Nonprofit Organizations

Copyright © 2015 by Polly K. Magnus, Author and Illustrator
Aurora, Colorado USA

All rights reserved. No part of this publication may be reproduced, distributed, or transmitted in any form or by any means, including photocopying, recording, or other electronic or mechanical methods, without the prior written permission of the publisher, except in the case of copying images for personal use, brief quotations embodied in critical reviews and certain other noncommercial uses permitted by copyright law.

Ordering Information:
Quantity sales. Special discounts are available on quantity purchases by corporations, associations, and others. Orders by U.S. trade bookstores and wholesalers. Please contact Amazon or visit www.amazon.com.

Printed in the United States of America

ISBN-13: 978-1518738074
ISBN-10: 1518738079

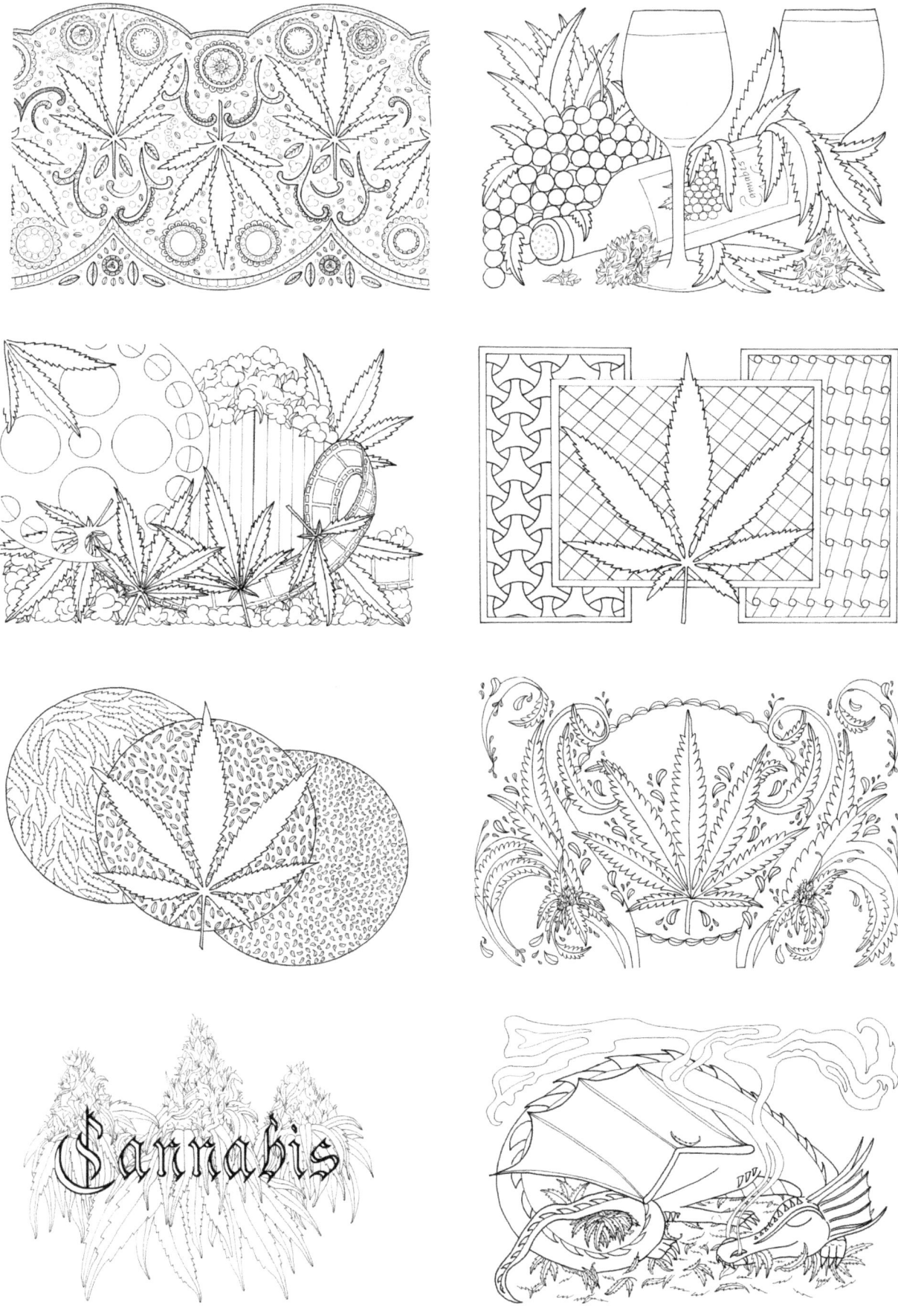

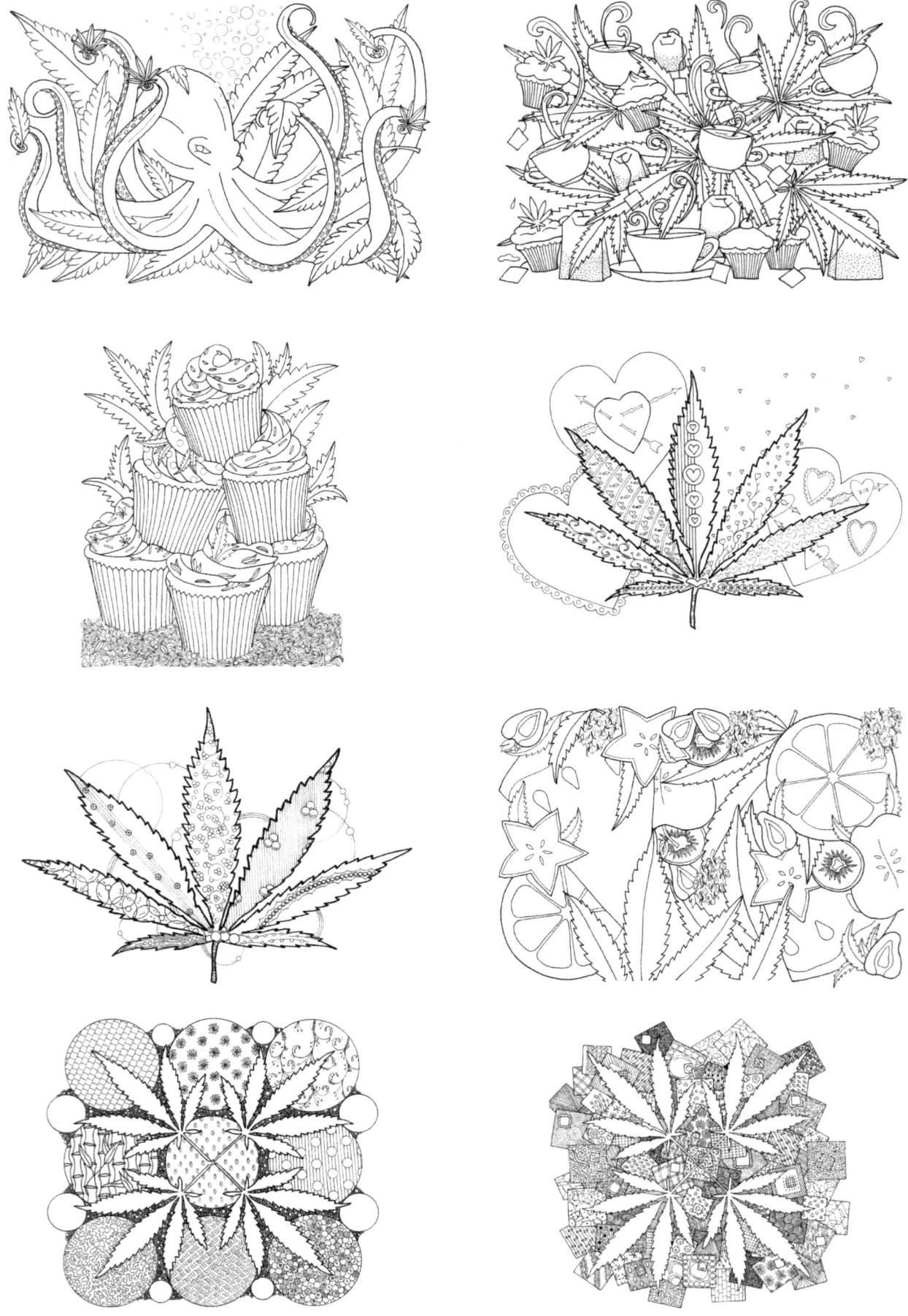

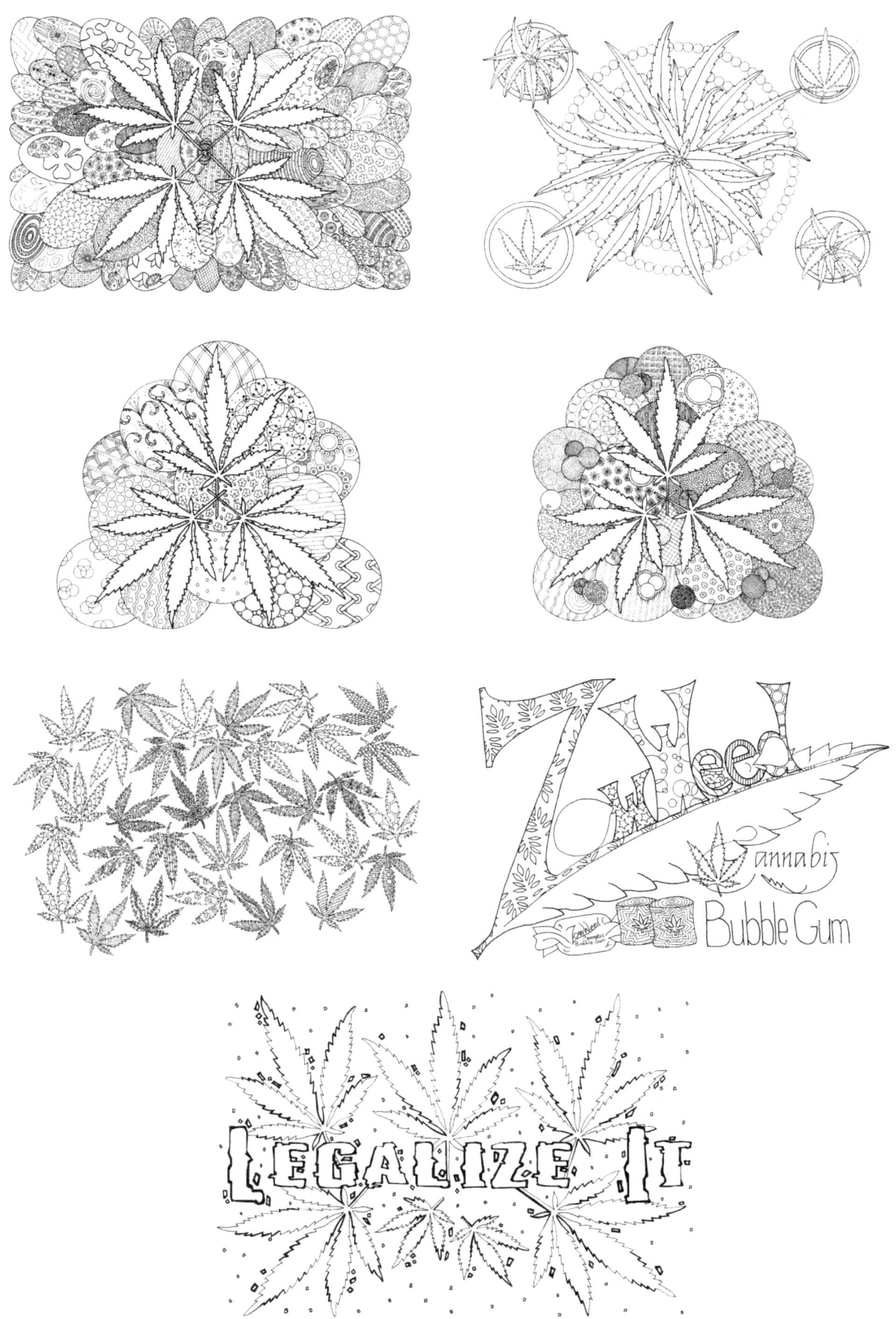

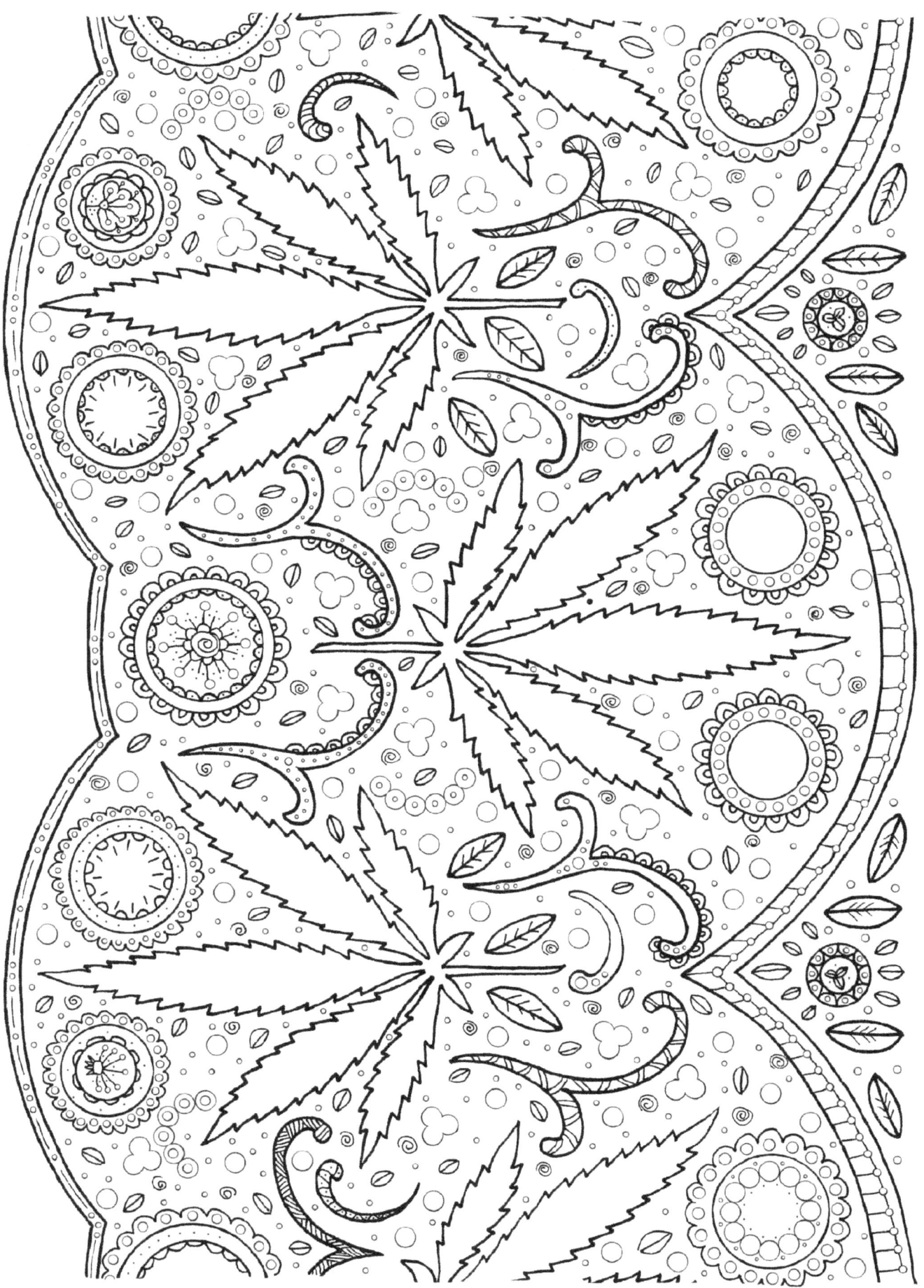

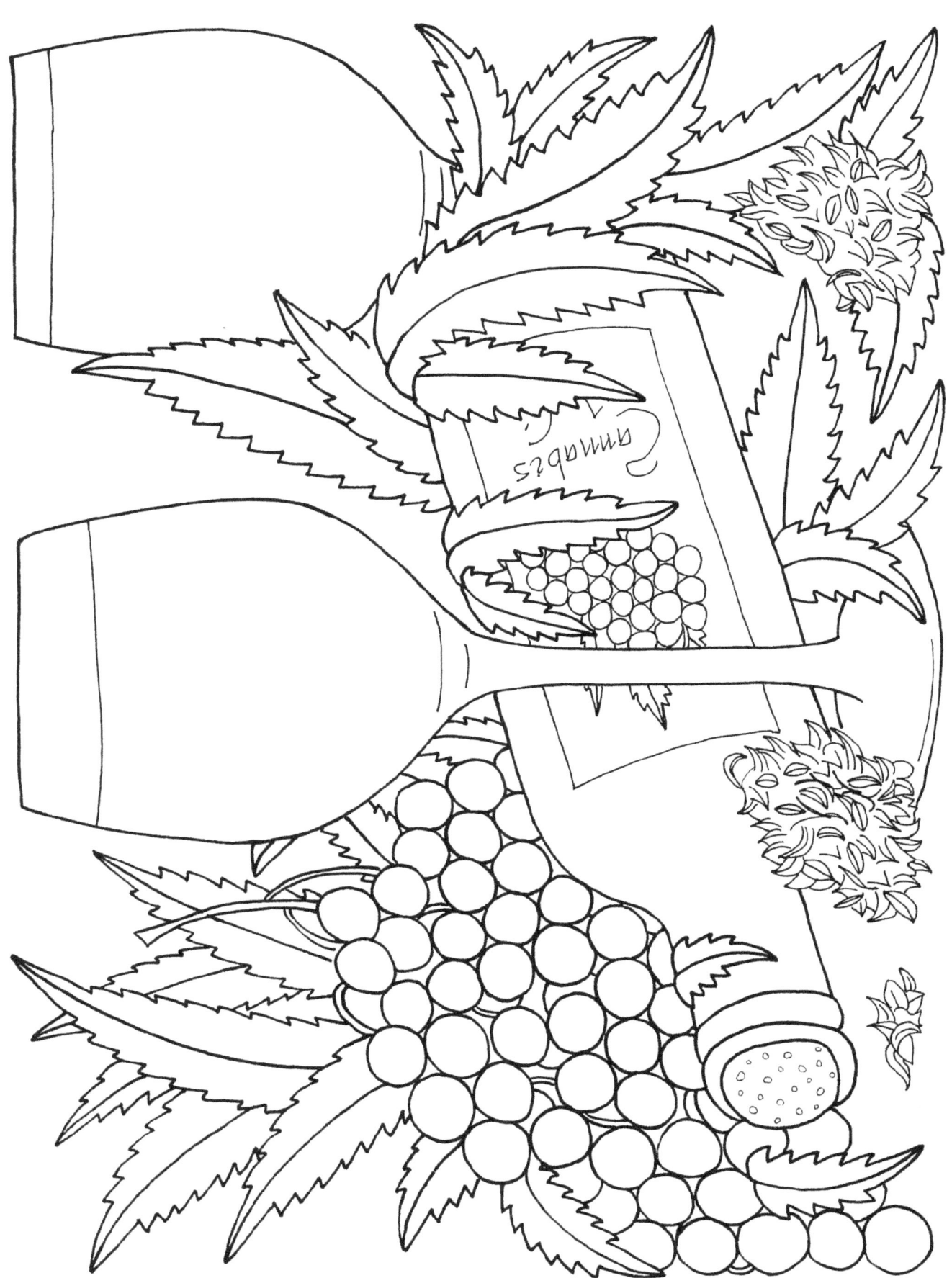

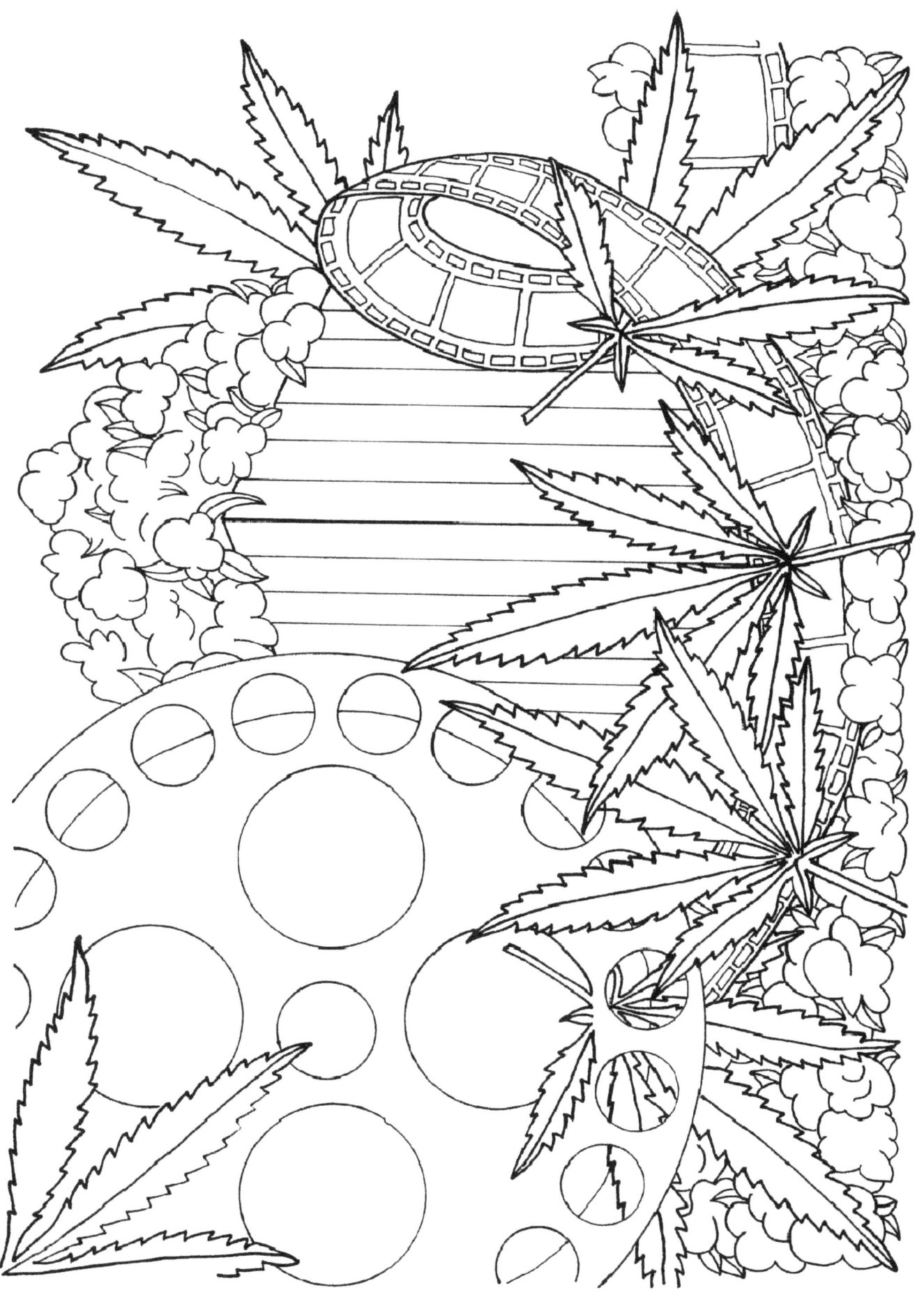

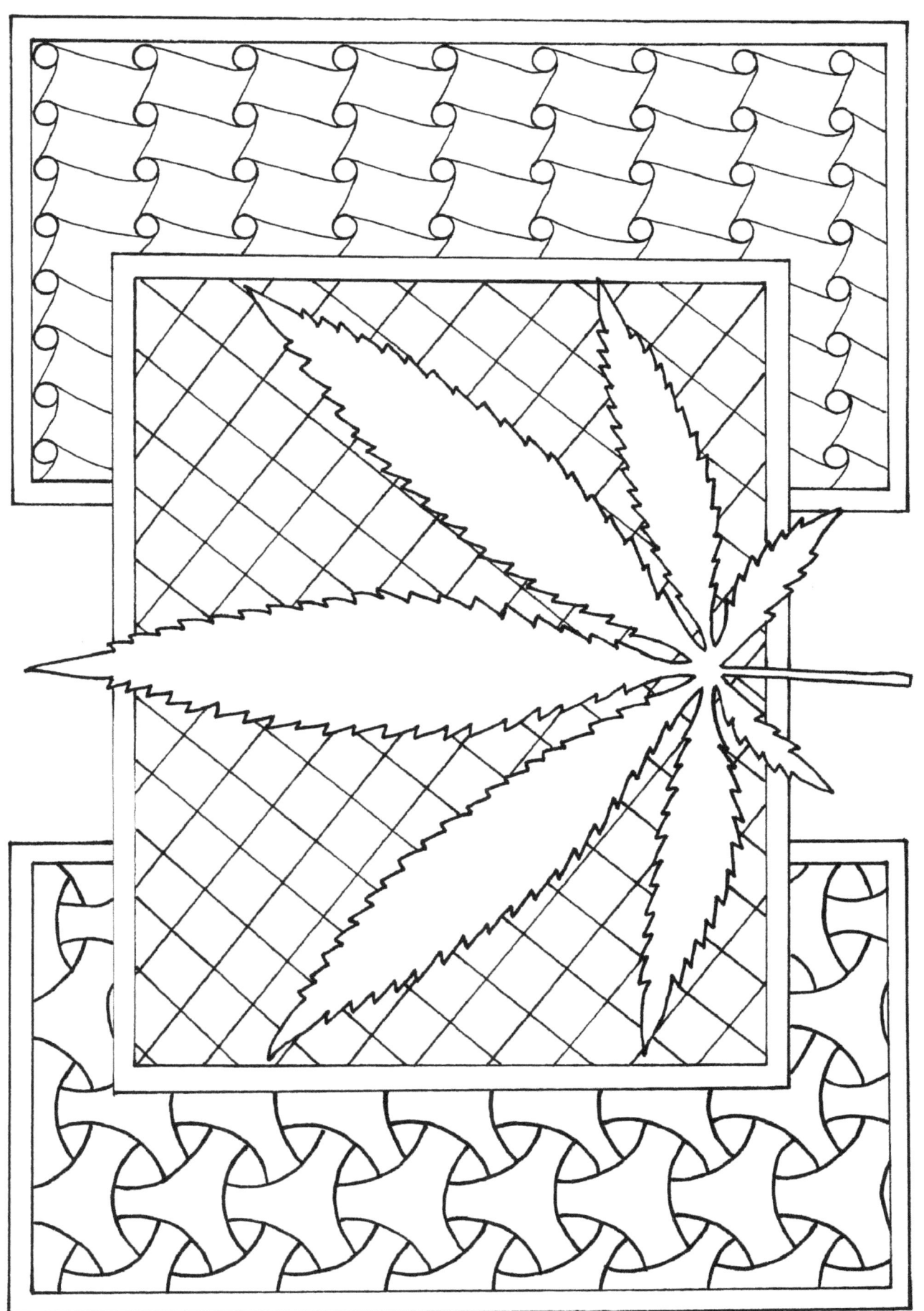

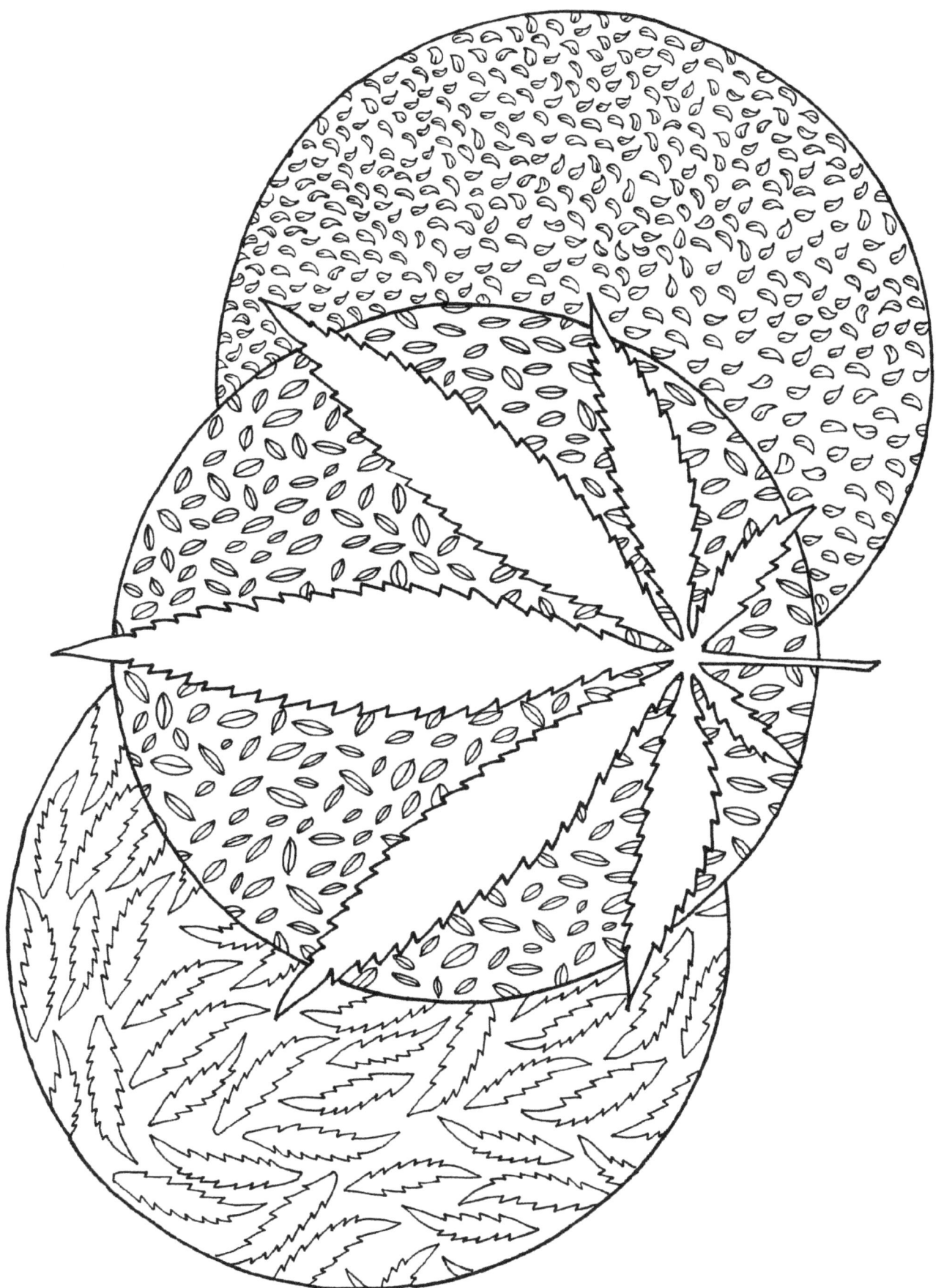

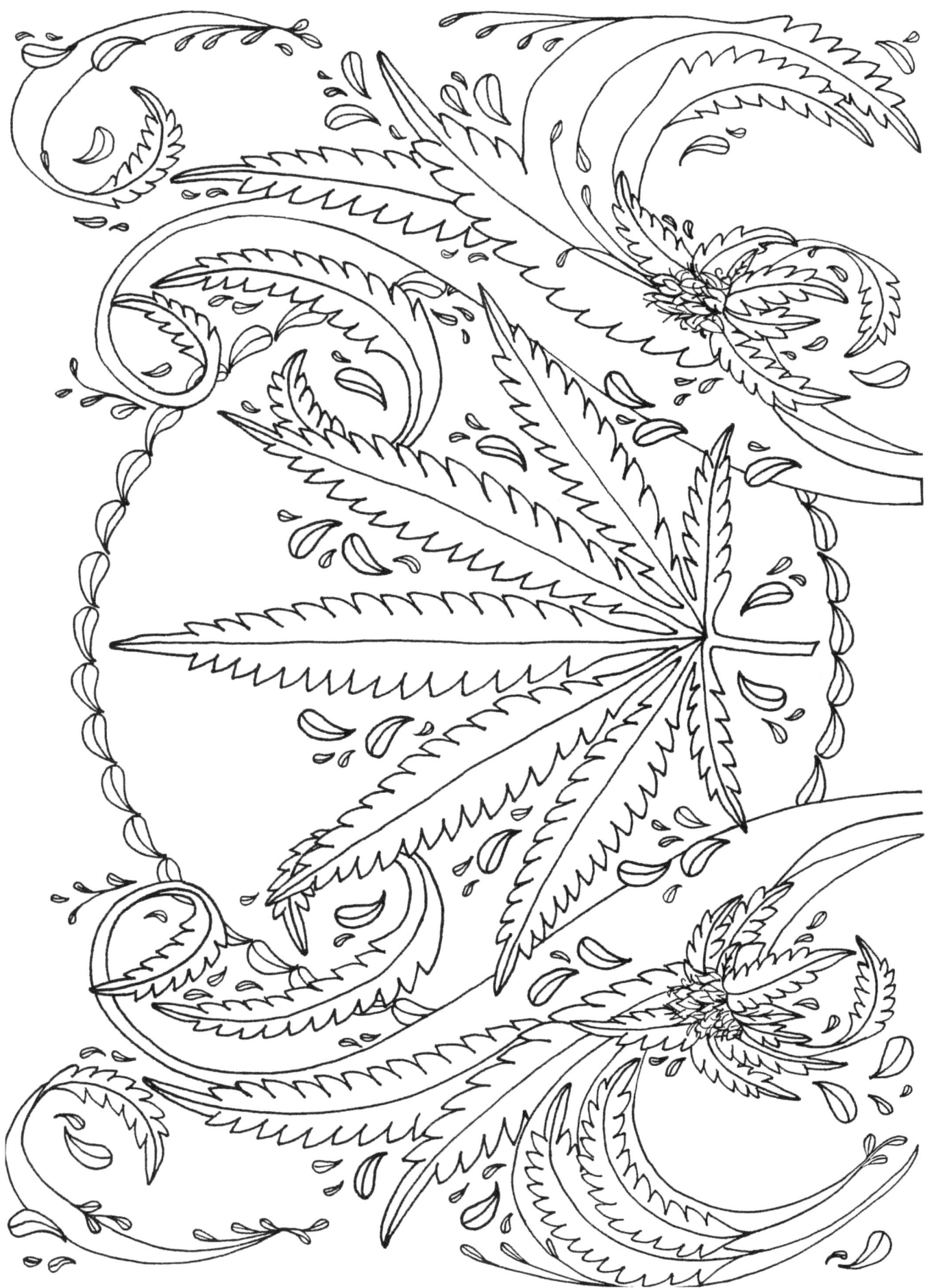

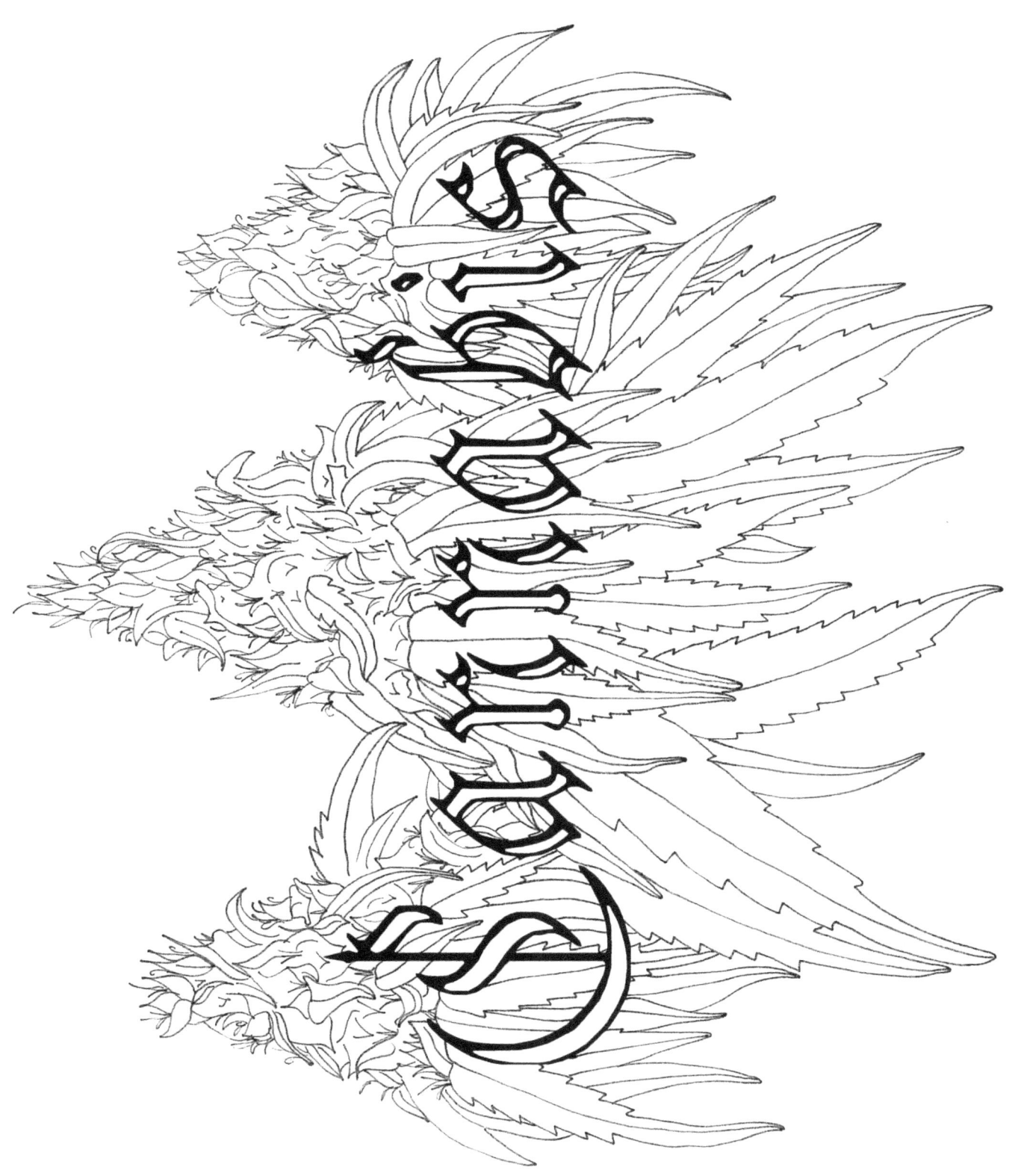

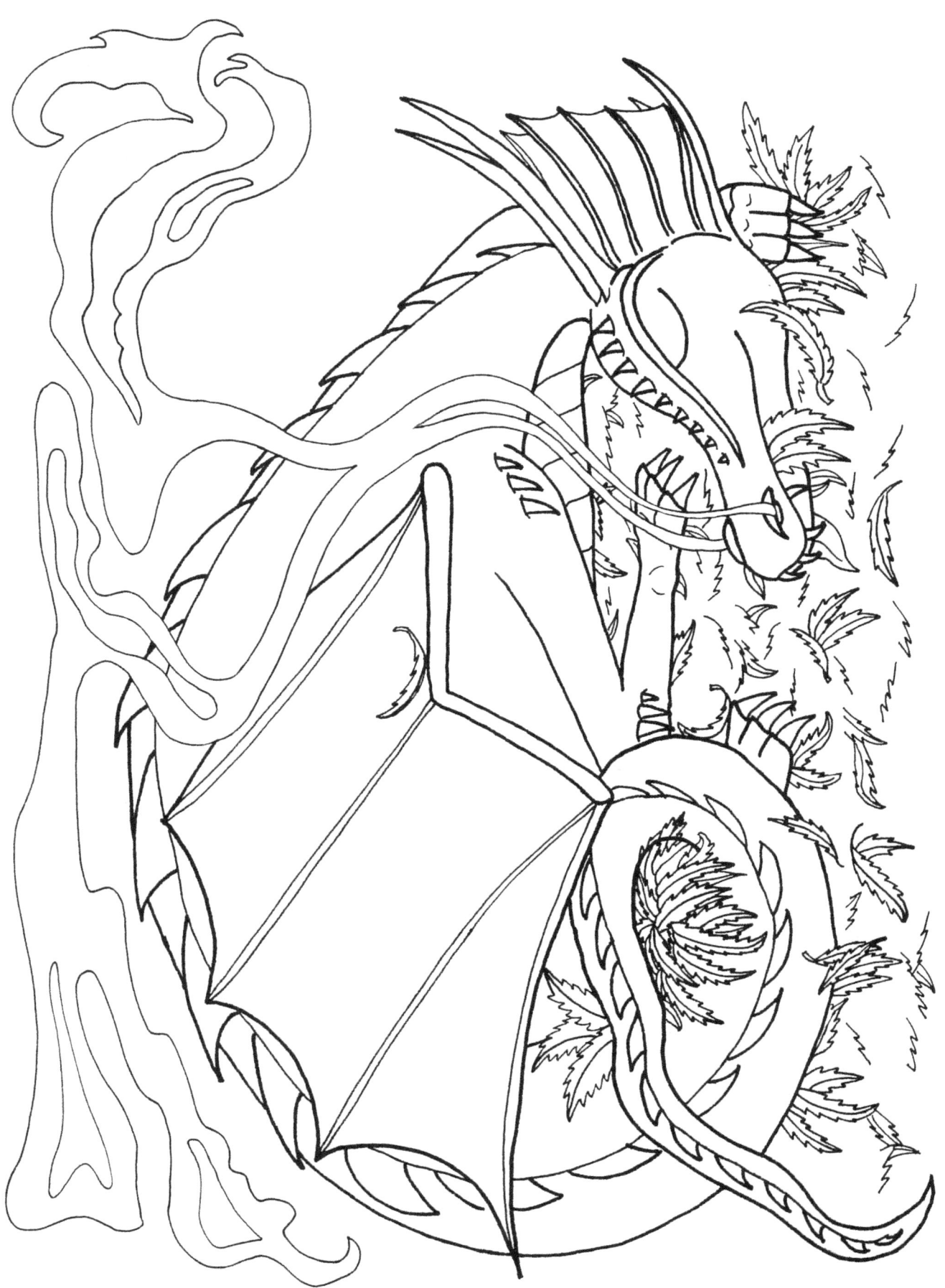

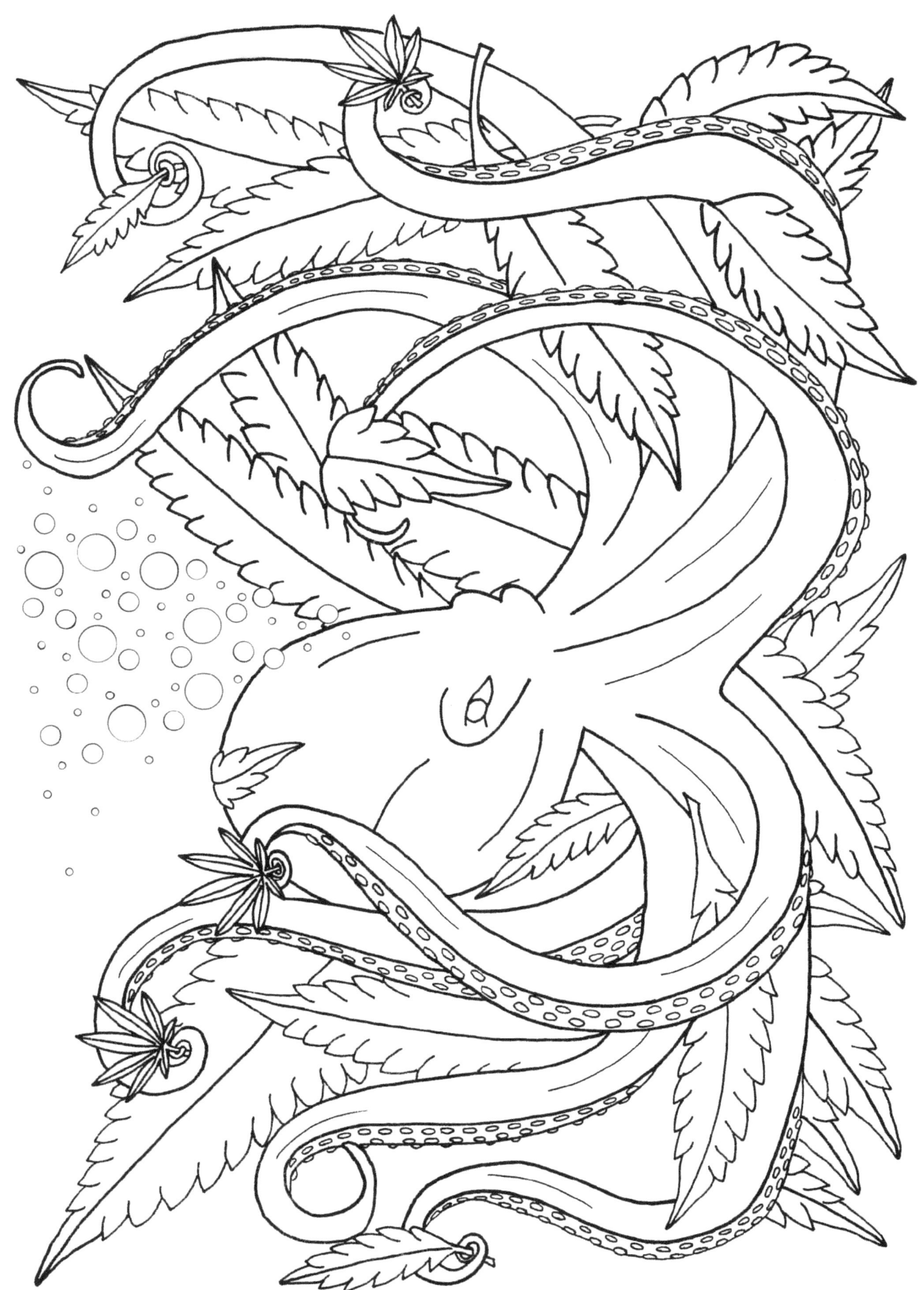

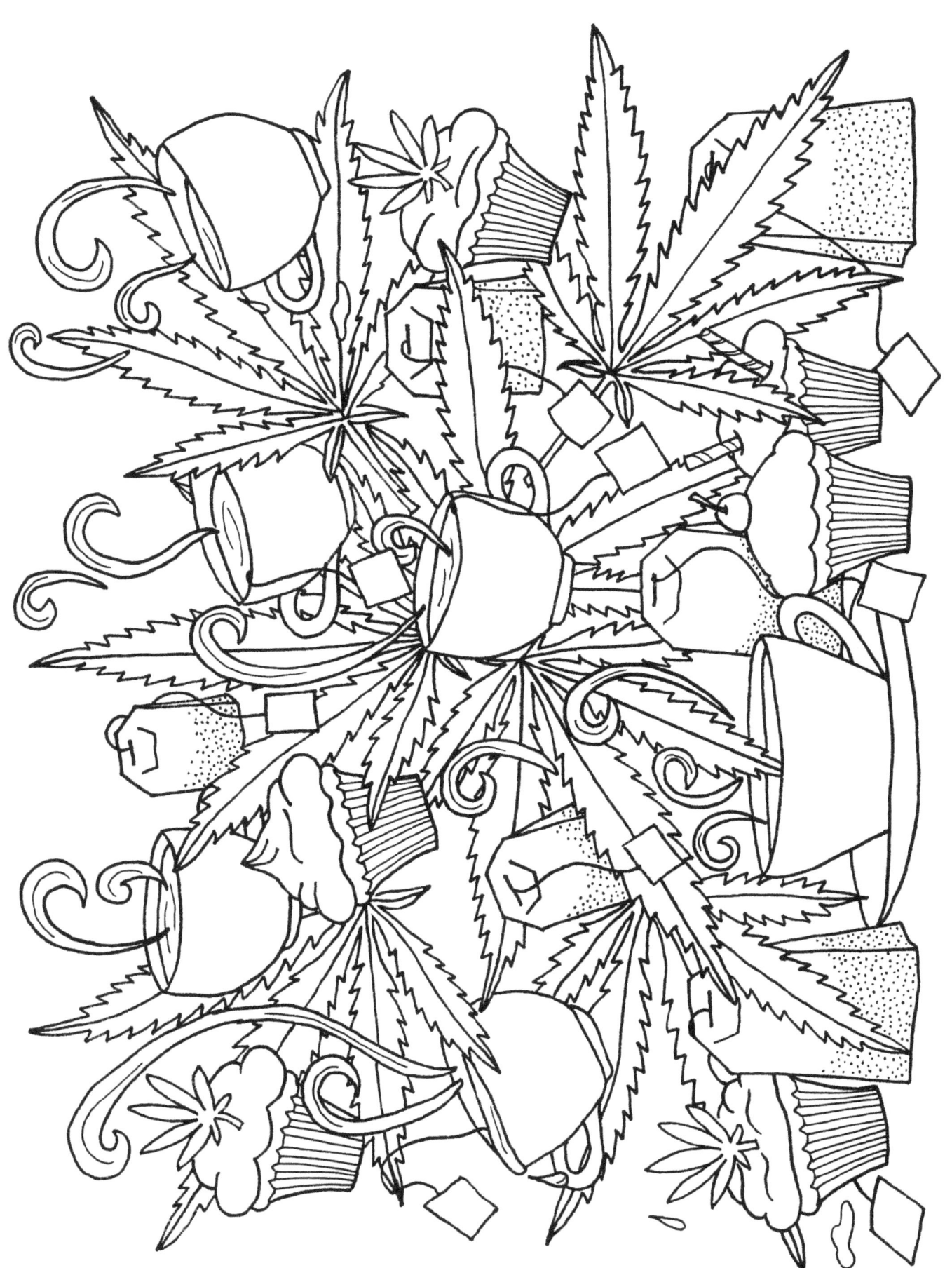

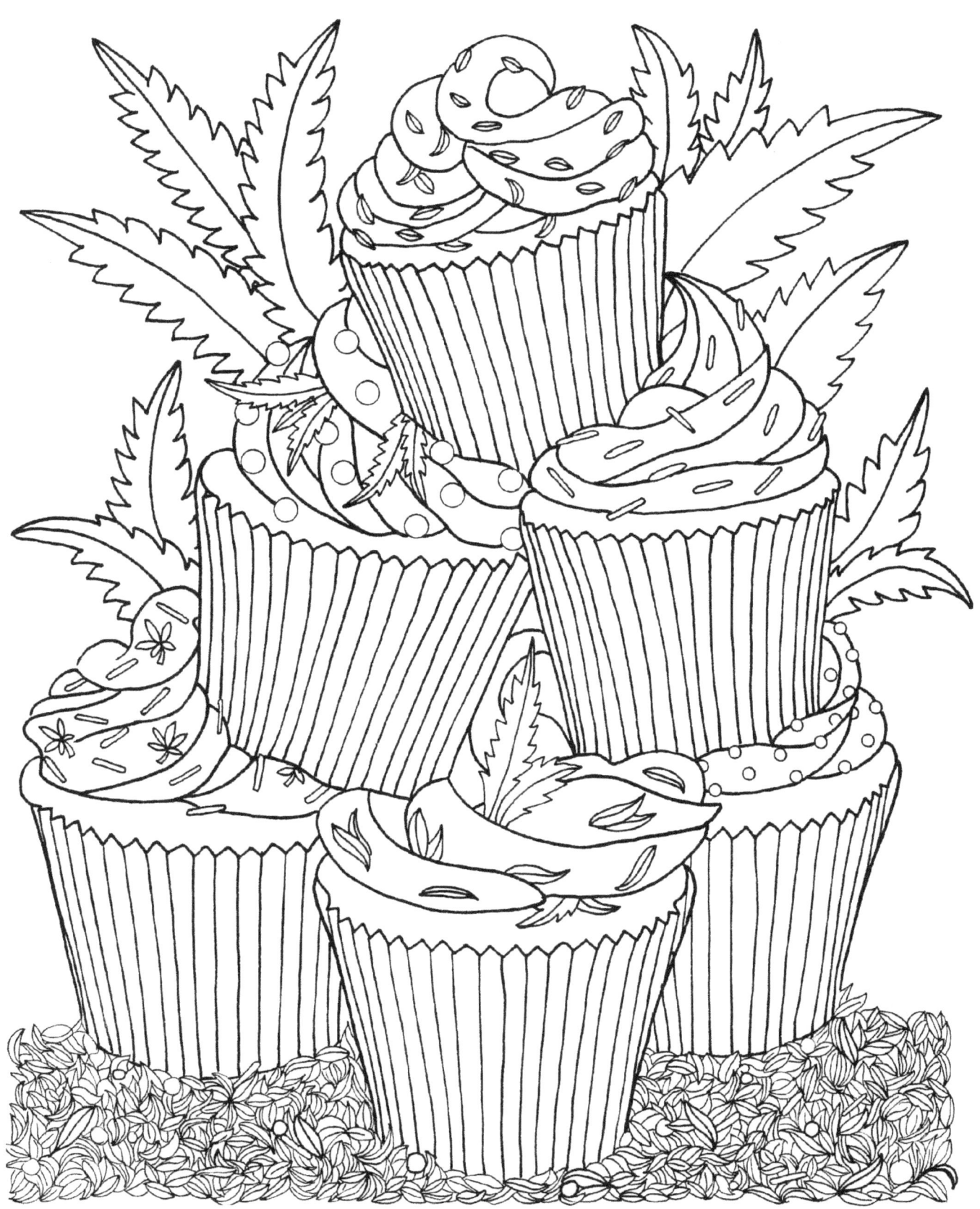

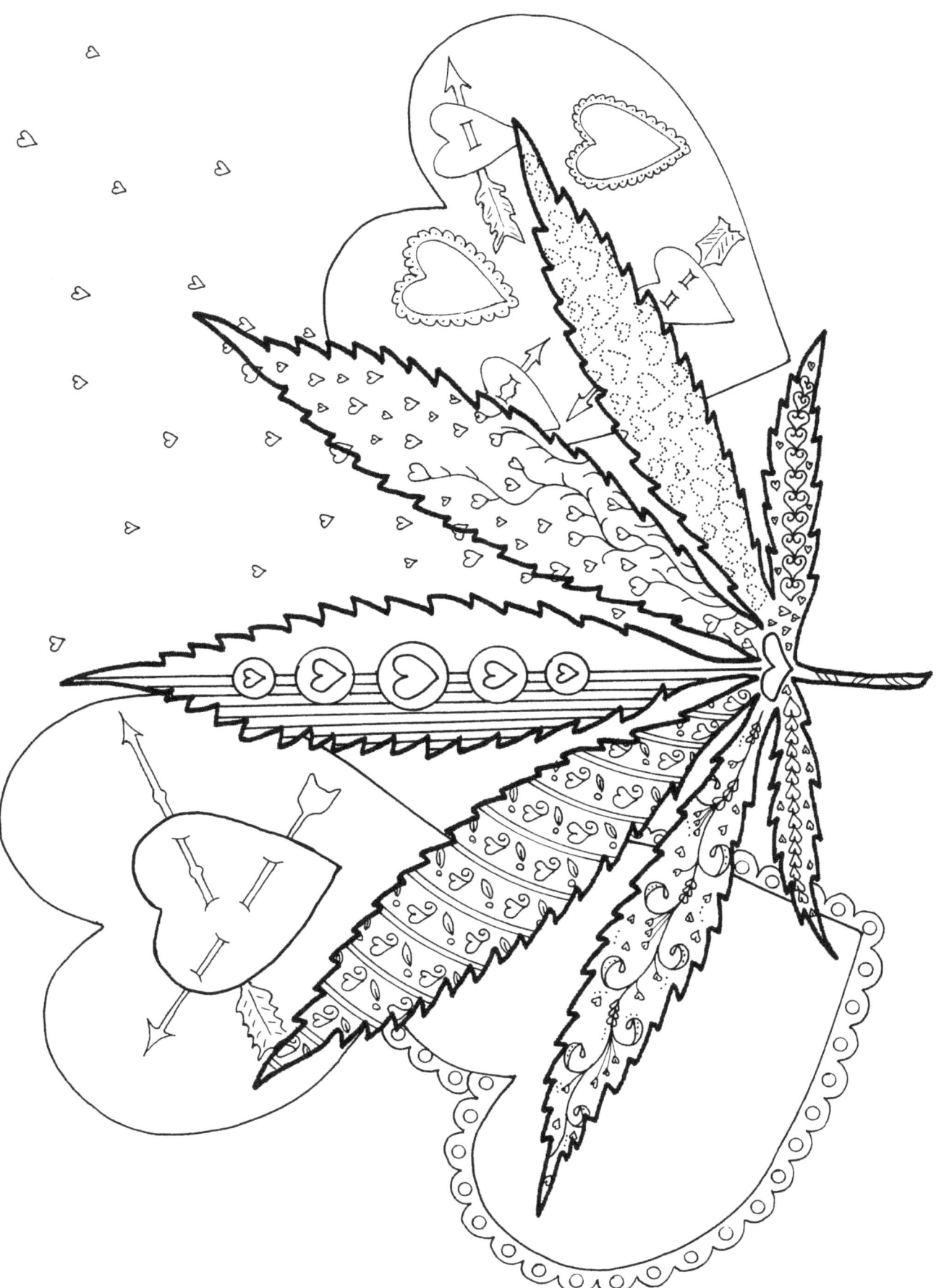

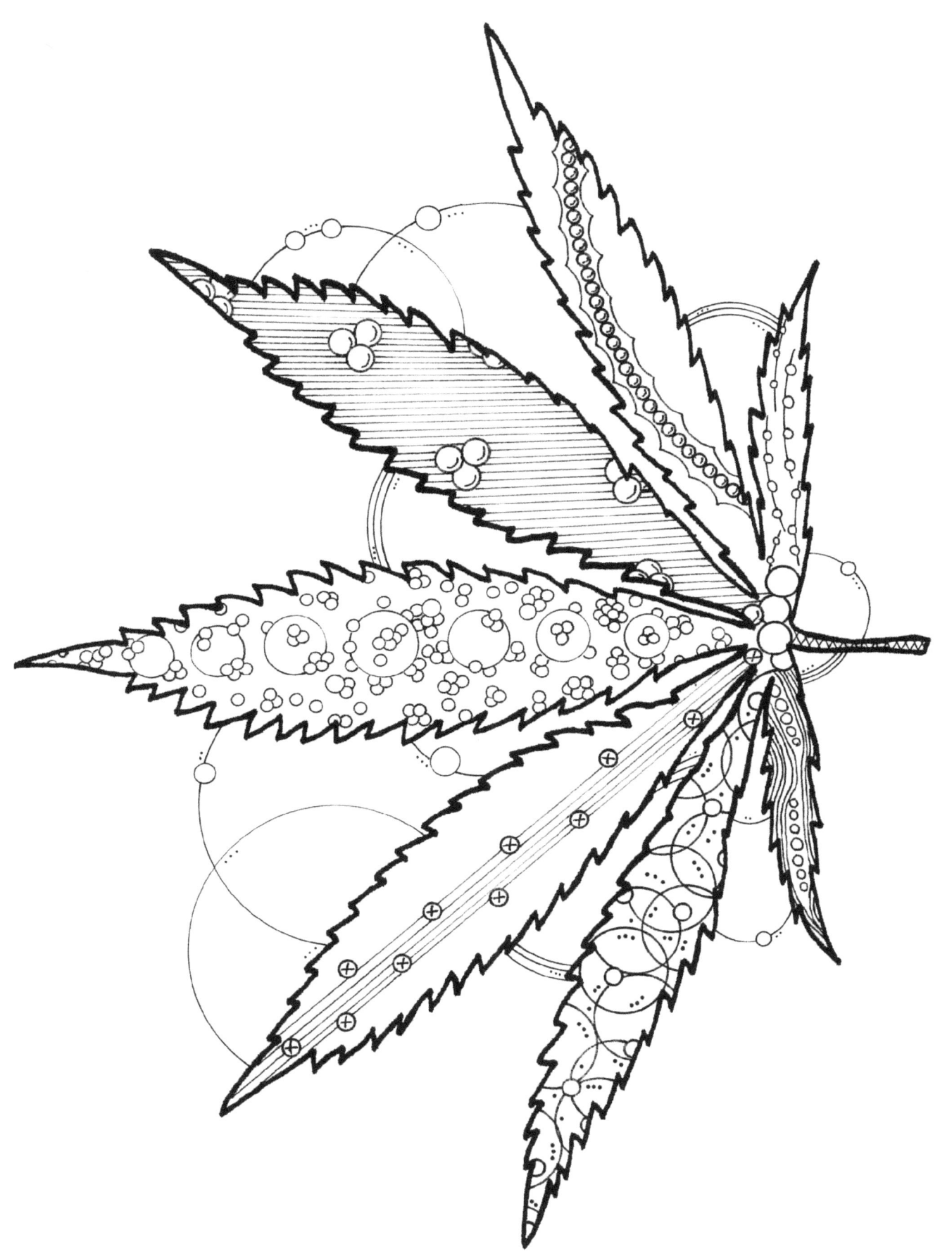

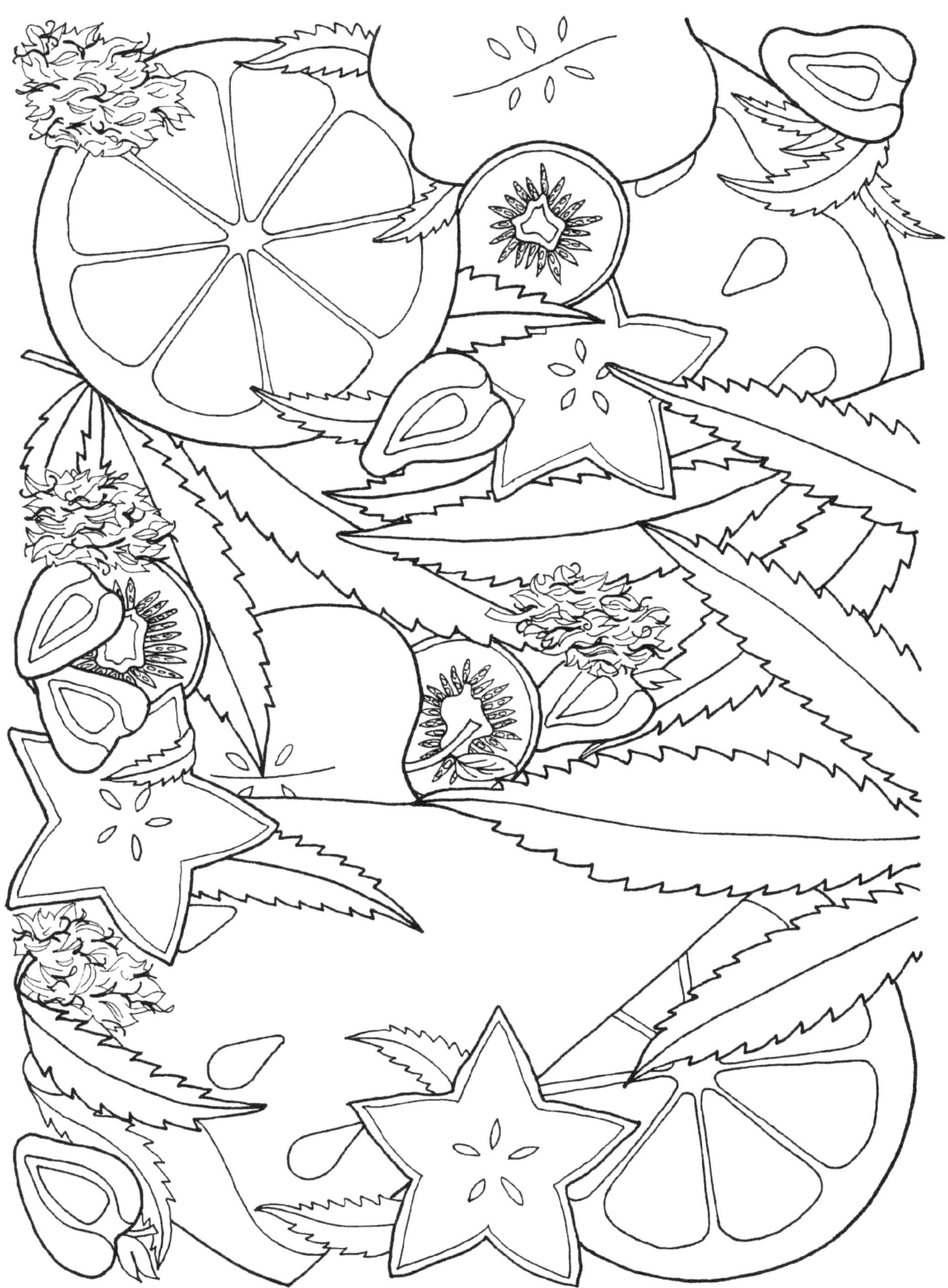

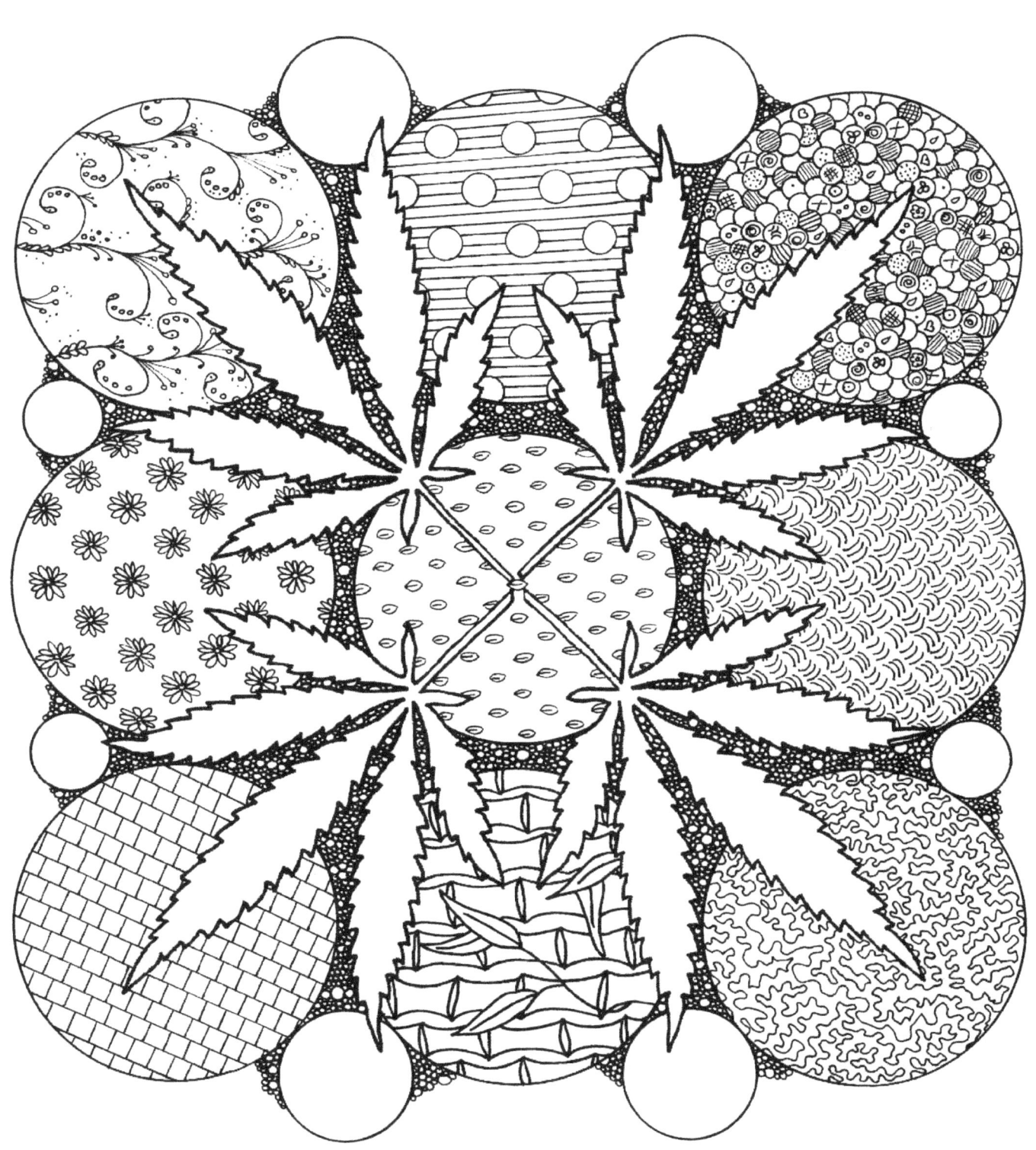

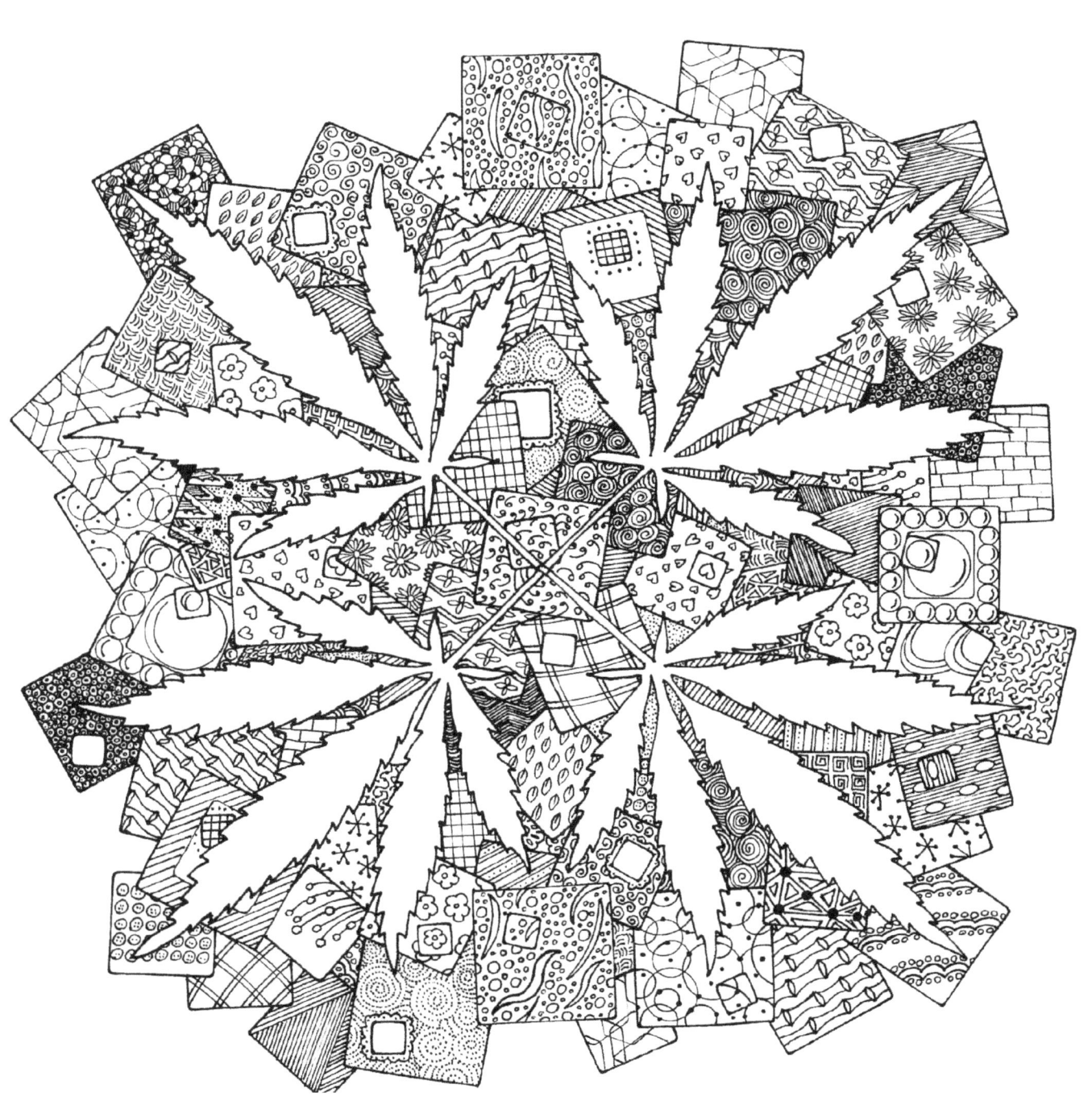

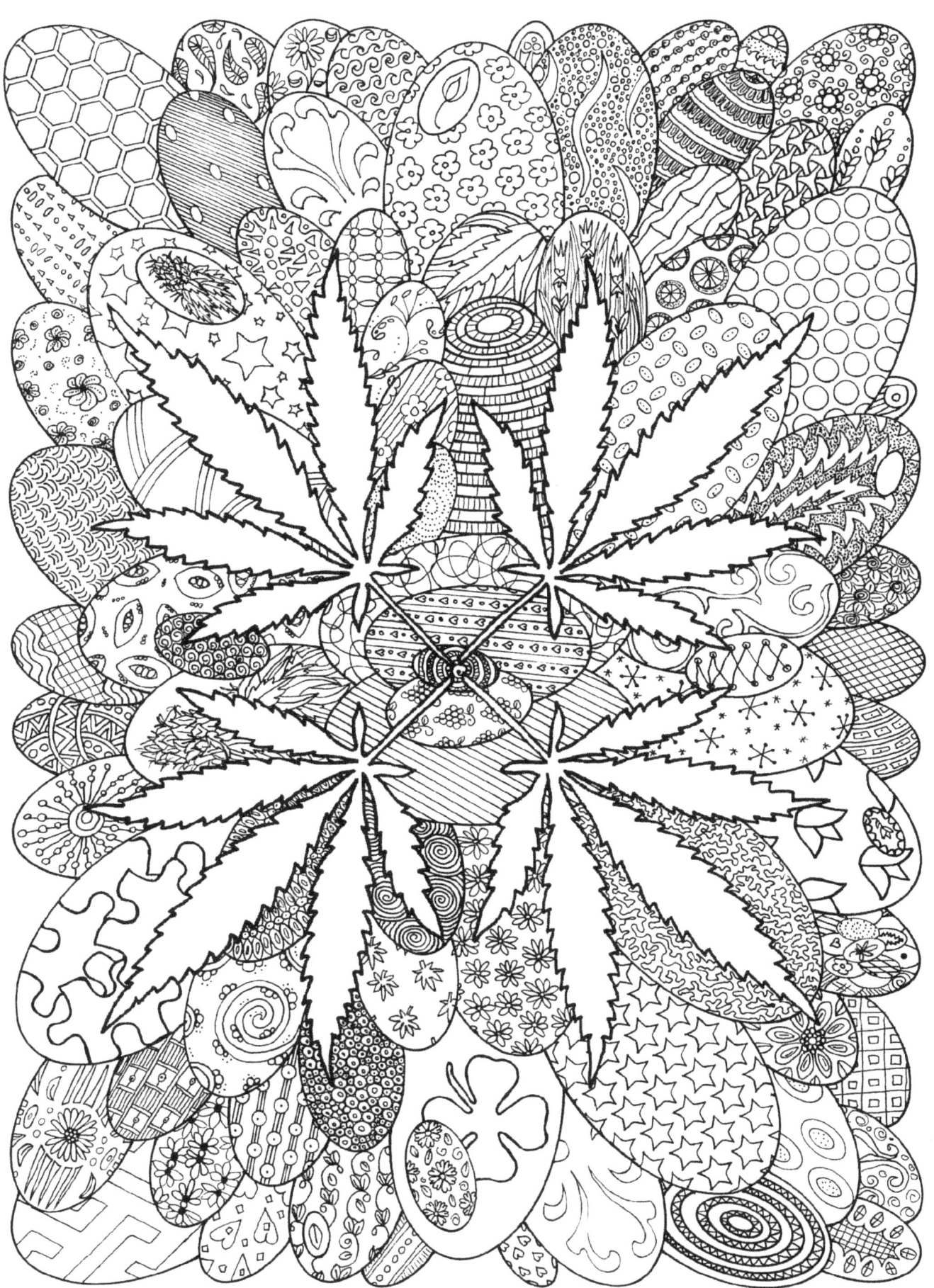

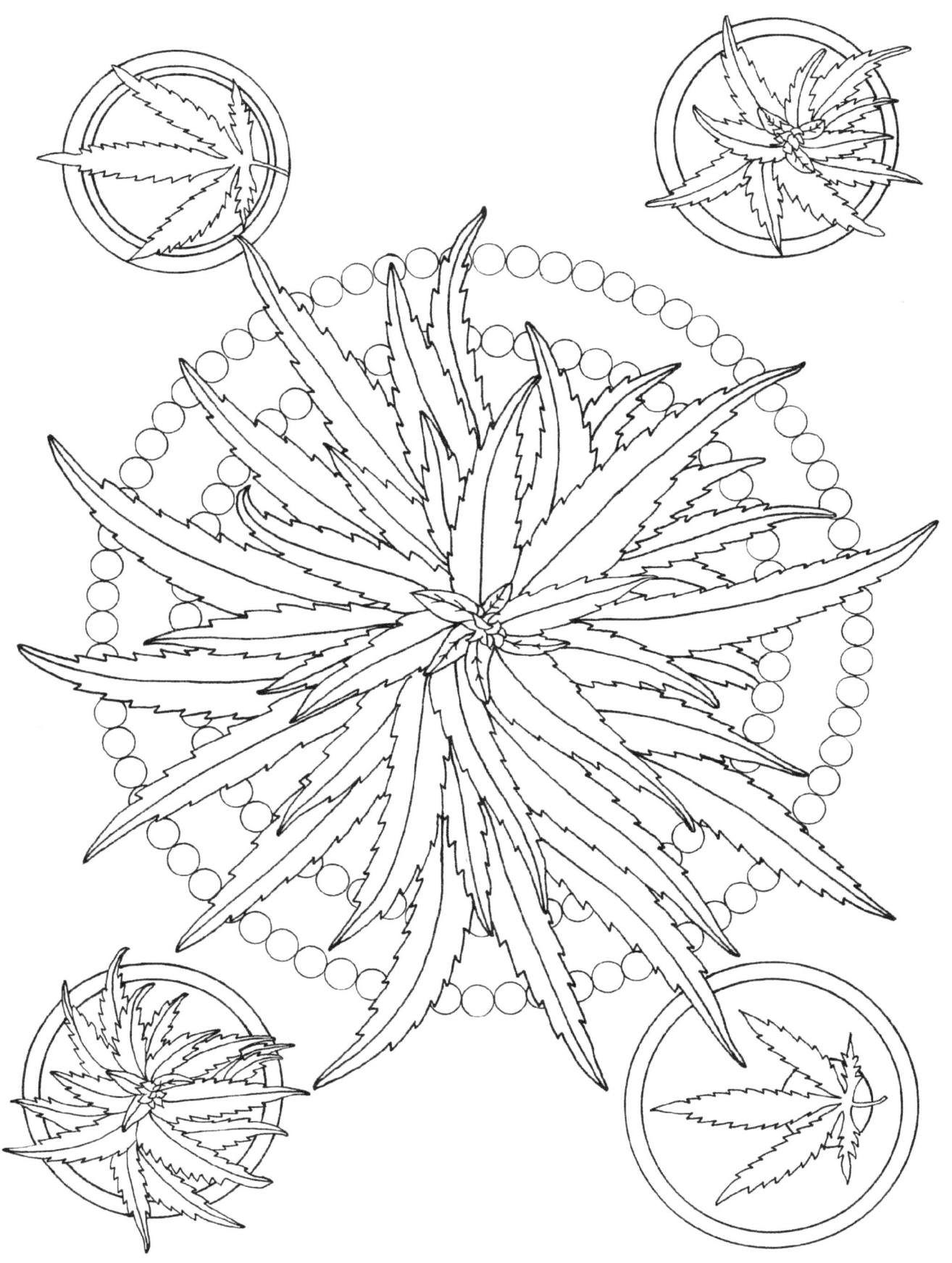

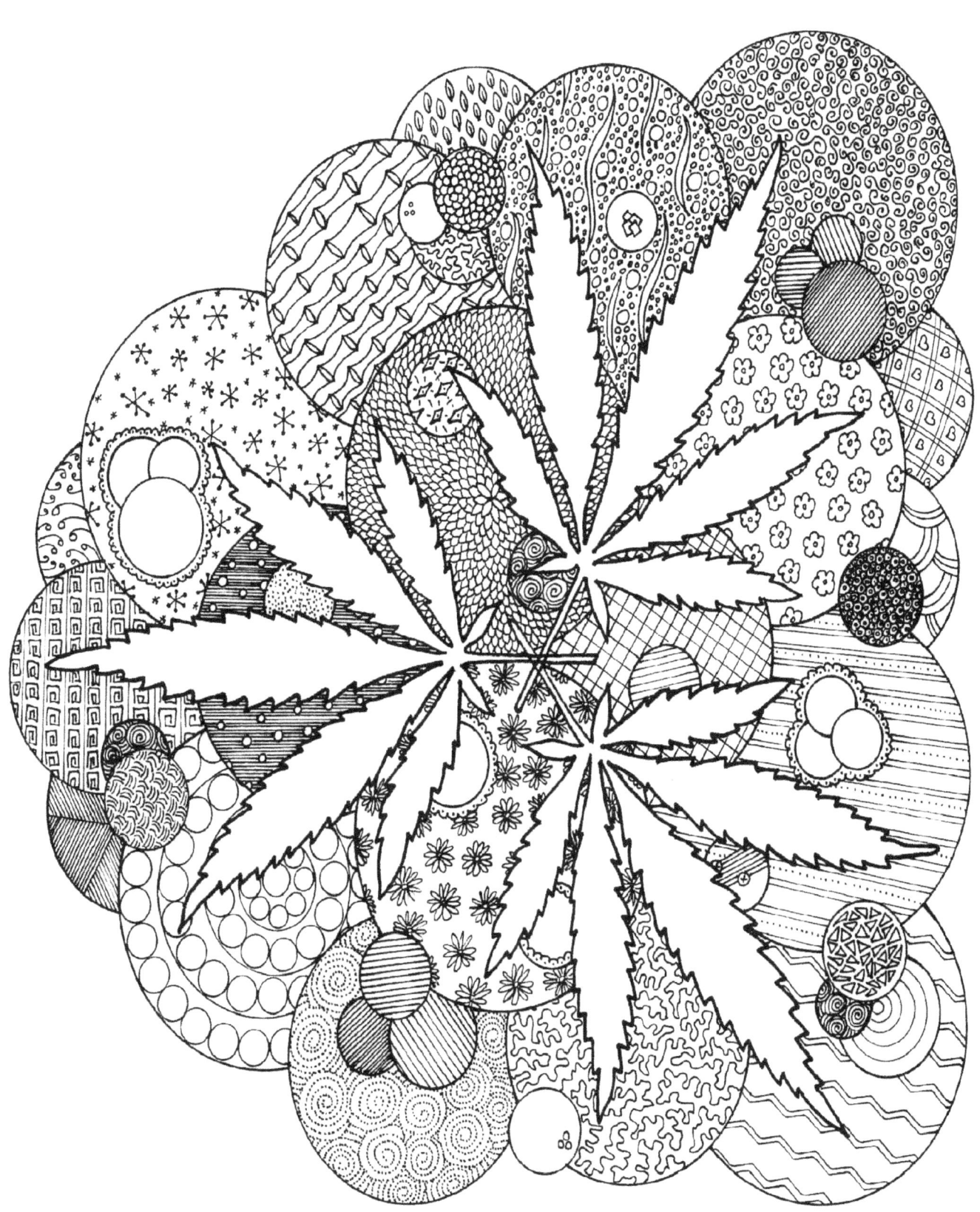

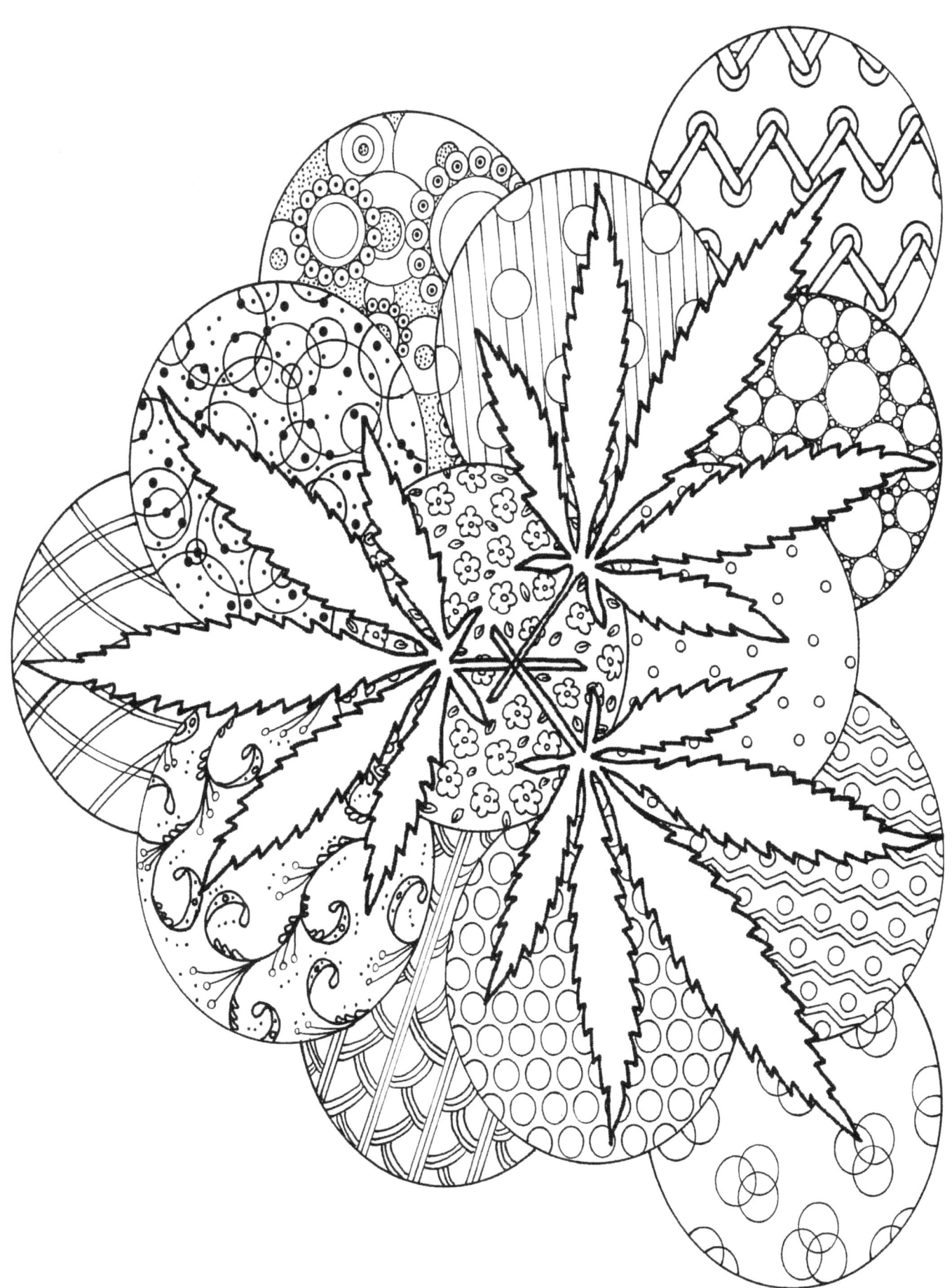

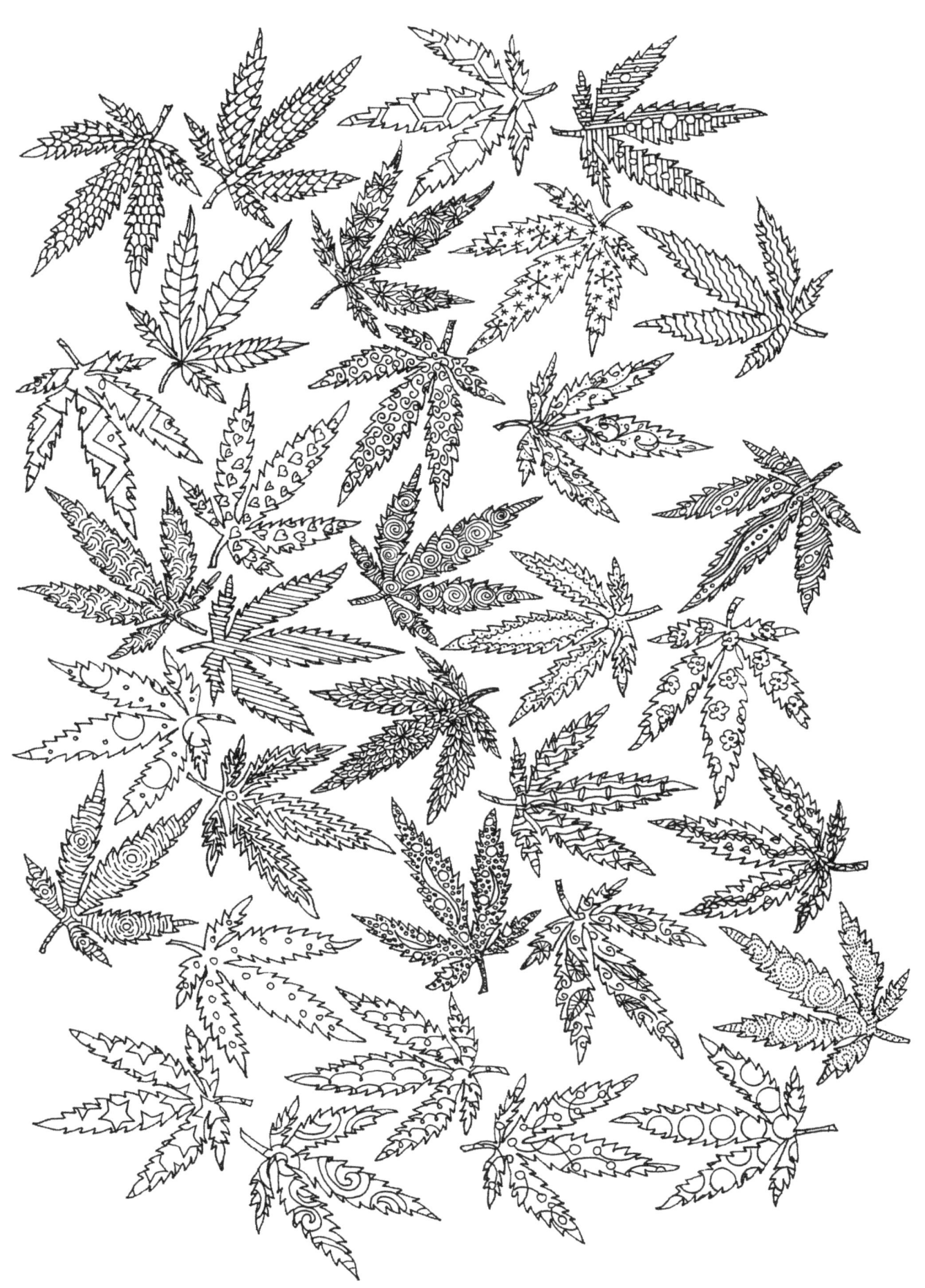

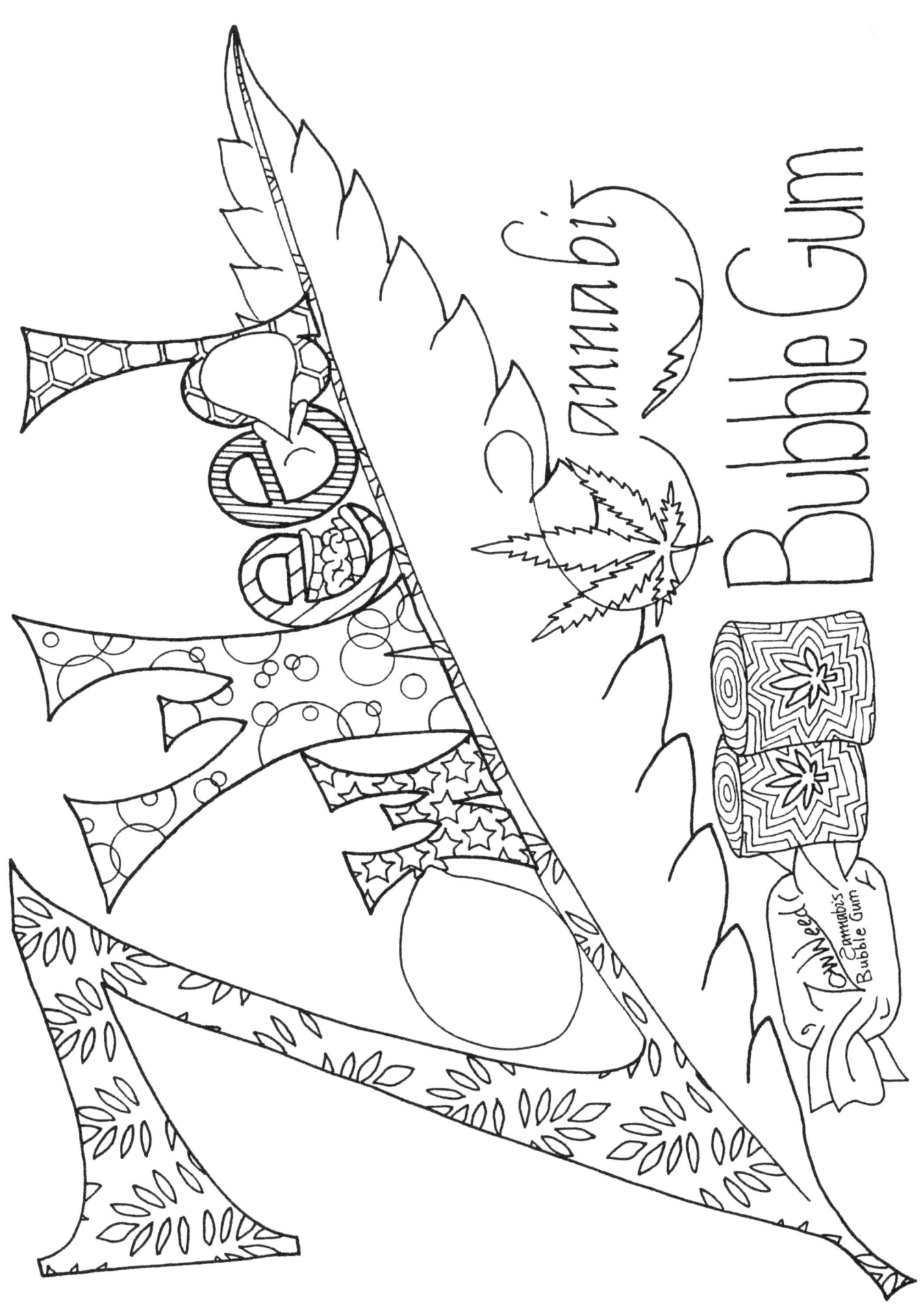

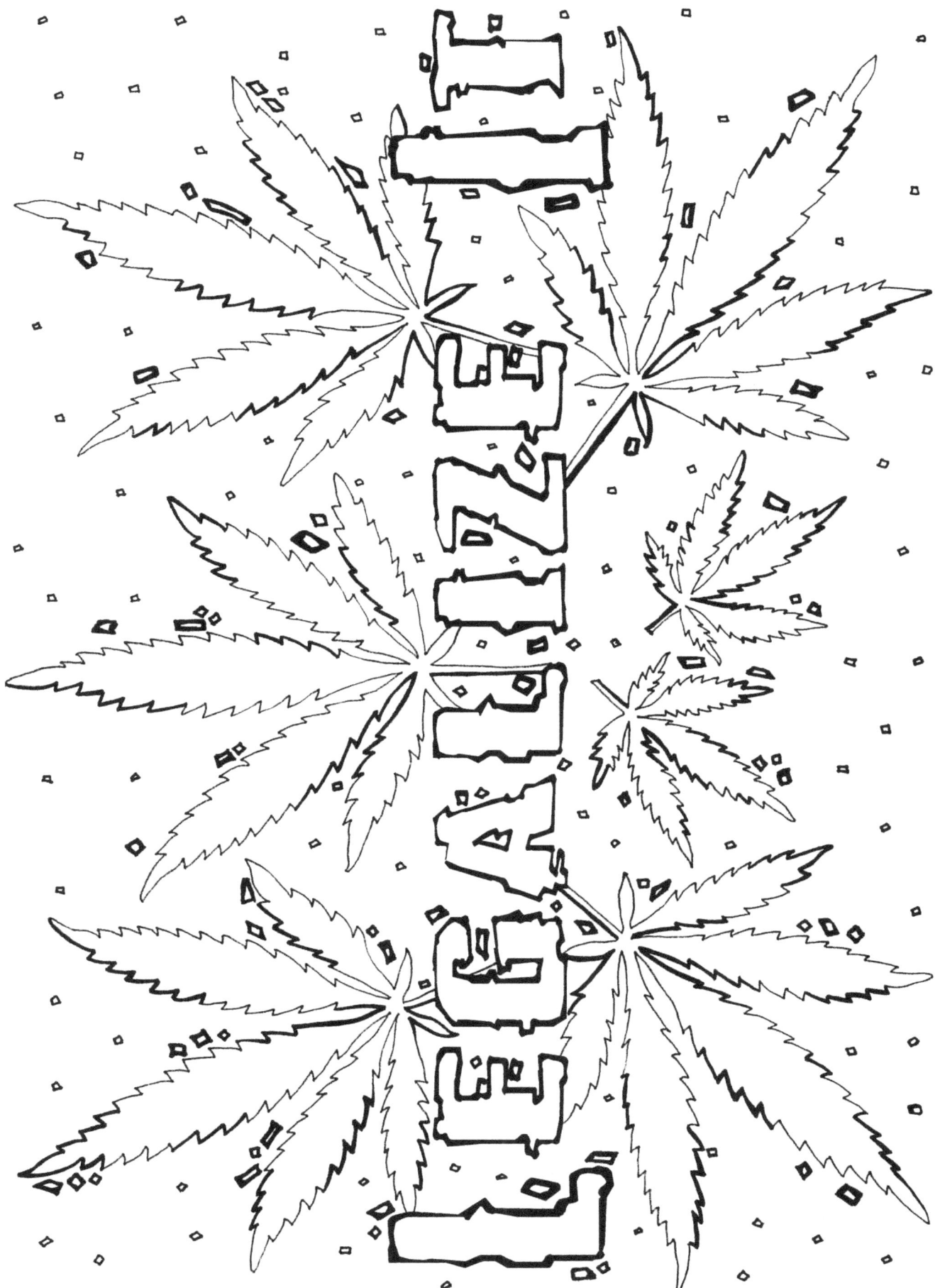

www.ingramcontent.com/pod-product-compliance
Lightning Source LLC
Chambersburg PA
CBHW080613180526

45168CB00007B/2900